Poems to Encourage & Challenge Believers in Christ Jesus

Janice Celestine

Editor: Jennifer Roderique

Cover design: Nigel-Wayne Williams

Dedication

This book of simple poems is dedicated to:

My husband, Michael Celestine

My sons, Nigel, Wesley and Steve Williams

Their wives, Kelly, Karen and Marlene Williams

My six grandchildren, Elijah, Micah, Kimiko,

Joshua, Kimani and Anna-Leigh Williams

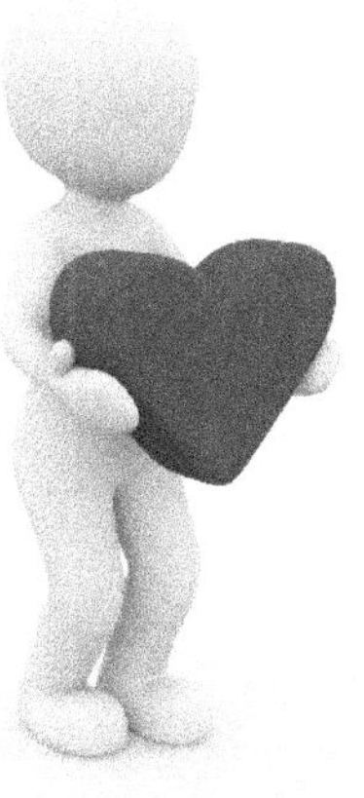

Table Of Contents

Foreword

To everything there is a season and a time for every activity under heaven" Ecclesiastes 3:1. Many are the plans of a man's heart but the Lord's timing is perfect.

The release of this book of poems by Elder Janice Celestine is very timely, because it was birthed from a cry deep within the heart of the writer to help encourage people especially youths.

This book was compiled through years of practical experiences which can now be used to help others who are caught in the valley of despair, guilt, depression, condemnation and fear. The writer, who herself has gone through trials and testing, is able to help others when they are faced with life struggles.

As her pastor, it is my firm conviction that this book of poems will truly challenge and encourage multitudes of Christians and non-Christians from all walks of life.

Apostle Irvin Celestine

HELPS and Deliverance Int'l Ministries

Introduction

I have always loved poetry, storytelling and drama since my childhood. This book of poems but uses the liberty allowed by poets to express themselves.

As a believer, we are sometimes faced with situations that try to defeat us. As the apostle Paul said, "we are pressed on each side."

The following poems were written to challenge and edify my brothers and sisters. It is written with such simplicity that a child can understand and share it.

My prayer is that it will be a blessing, a source of edification and encouragement to the readers.

Keep standing, my brethren!

Be Encouraged

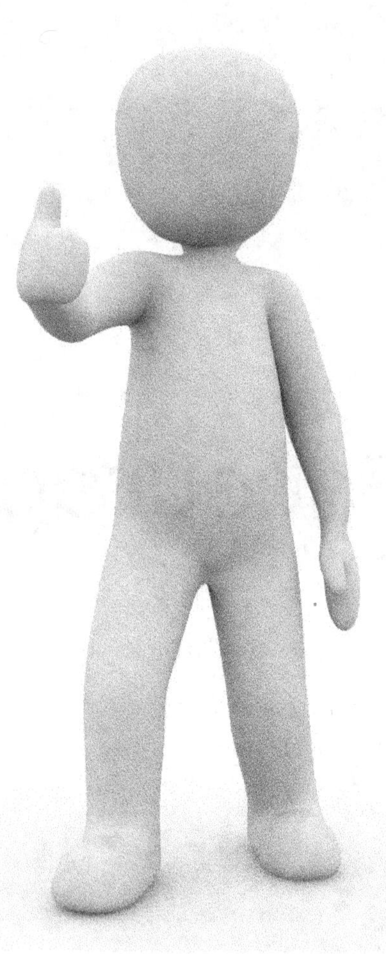

DO A WORK IN ME

Count it all joy when you fall into temptation

Tells us this Christian life is not all fun

No playing games when God's word is told

For He wants to bring us through as very fine gold

So, stop complaining when things are tough

God allows us just what is enough

Instead, your prayer or plea should be

"Lord, do a work in me"

When your bread basket is all bare

And you don't have the luxury for which you care

When your money is low

On your face it shouldn't show

When your clothes are the same ones you wear all the time

You long to see others but can't see a dime

When the fire is hot, hot

God is still there with you but

Instead of saying, 'Lord look the trouble I see

Say instead "Lord, do a work in me"

Victory, victory is easy to say

When everything is going our way

Remember in everything give thanks

For in happiness or sadness God is still working His plans

He promised never to leave us for a single day

If you believe that then smile and say

Lord, I really don't understand it all

But you are with me whether I stand or fall

Open my eyes that I may see

That you are doing a work in me

When your friends say they forgive you

But feed you with a long handle spoon

When they talk behind your back, morning, night and noon

Don't despair, God is still there

Don't worry your head

Pray for them instead

God is talking you through this so that self will die

So that for everything you will not cry

When the waves are raging, get on your knee

And say "Lord, do a work in me!"

Remember Abraham was asked to kill his son Isaac

How many would have said that was Satan's attack

And Joseph's brothers sold him as a slave

But he did not complain rant or rave

God took him through to the very end

He ended up a ruler in Egypt my friend

Remember all things work for the Christian good

If you never learn that verse, I think now you should

So, when in pain, don't be ashamed

Do a work in me Lord is what to proclaim

I know God is still working on all of us

Even at time all we do is fuss

Let's not be weary in well doing my friend

Keep your eyes on Jesus to the very end

And whatever is needful He will take us through

Be sure, sure, sure He is still working on you

So together we can all shout with glee

"Lord, continue to work in me"

ENTERING THE REST OF GOD

There is a place of rest in God, you know
Those who have entered in, their lives show
Hebrews chapter 4 verse 3 makes it absolutely clear
Why the Israelites did not enter, so have a care
God swore that they will not enter His rest
They made Him very angry as they flunked every test
Through murmuring complaining and fault-finding
Seeing and hearing, yet being rebellious and provoking
These are the same people who crossed the Red Sea
As Moses lifted his rod and gave them victory

They did not enter into God's rest, no doubt
Because their unbelief had shut them out
They were unwilling to trust in and rely on God
Following their example, we cannot afford
We need to listen to God's word and obey His instructions
To avoid staying outside of God's rest unto damnation
Experiencing God's rest will tell you are in faith
Once you remain there you will enter the pearly gate

Know that God is a rewarder of them that seek Him

Earnestly and diligently from their hearts within

Frustration occurs when you try to do only what God can

Let you soul rest in God, He's able man

Being in God's rest is not just resting physically

But resting in confidence in God's ability

To take care of everything that goes on in your life

While your mind, will and emotions are at peace not strife

God desires that we live at peace and in His rest

Quit trying to control things and pass every test

When you feel frustrated or upset

Or you lose your peace, your joy and only fret

Ask yourself, are you believing in God's word

That tells us never to worry, God is in control?

I advise you to count your blessings instead

Name them one by one and don't dread

He's still the great I AM be sure

Whatever He did for you before, there is still more

Remember even your test is tailor made for you

To prove you believe God, always give Him His due

Believers when you enter God's rest

You'll have peace that passes understanding in every test

Joy unspeakable and full of glory

Having a calm and peaceful heart, never a worry

You are guaranteed a love that is complete

And so, all of Satan's plans you will defeat

Enter into His blessed rest today

Live in obedience and stay that way

So that when the final drum roll

You will be with Jesus not in the devil's hold

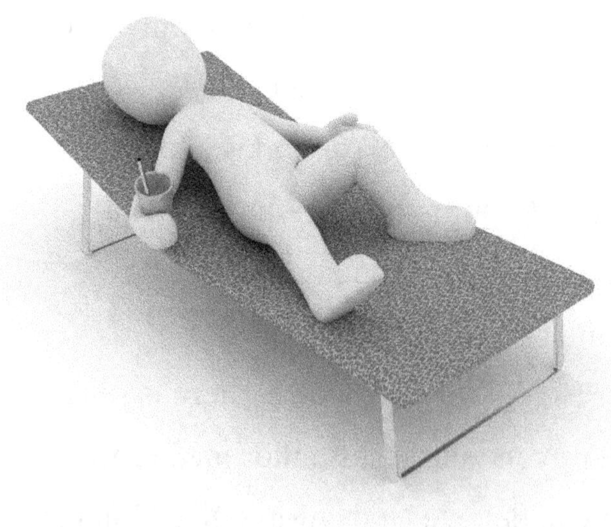

CREATION DECLARES THE GLORY OF GOD

When was the last time you scrutinised creation

Noting the variety of birds that flies in the heavens?

And that they sing different songs too

Take time to listen it will amaze you

Our Great God created them all

And though some things changed after the fall

The creativity of God can still be seen

In the beauty, colour, and songs of birds to their maker
supreme

Who taught the eagles how to fly?

As they make great heights in the sky

Their wings flap very little as they soar

Conserving energy as they gain height more and more

Bald eagles can fly to an altitude of 10,000 feet

Our awesome God's creativity is impossible to beat

Isaiah says if we wait on the Lord we will not flop

But our strength will be renewed and we will mount up

Yes, mount up with wings like the eagles, real high

Run and not be weary, walk and not faint nor die

The human body too is really magnificent

The mechanics of the eyes speaks of Gods intelligence

Cameras are patterned from the eyes we possess

That beholds God's creation and aren't blessed?

The lens in the eyes and camera functions the same

God is amazing no wonder He has such fame

Computers we must always remember

Are blueprints of the brain that God designed He is superior

Just as airplane are fashioned like the birds

The body of mankind is superb to behold

The way human beings are formed is incredible

Scientists have recorded the process and they marvel

As the sperm and the egg come together and multiply

It is mind boggling to understand the One in the sky

God says He knitted us together in our mothers' womb

As Psalm 139 informs revealing from the womb to the tomb

TREASURES TO REMEMBER

Hey you, yes you my sister and brother

Here are some important things to remember

If you take this advice seriously

You will love and not offend or be offended anybody

Apart from that your faith will grow

And your changed renewed mind will show

That you have surely grown closer to God

Living with love joy and the peace God's kingdom affords

These verses I have kept close to my heart

As a young believer from the very start

It has resulted in my spiritual growth yes

In spite of my mistakes, I remain blessed

These reminders are by no means all you need to know

But they are great keys to help you glow

When trouble seem to threaten on every side

In Joshua 1:5 is where you should abide

Our loving God will not leave you nor forsake you

Not just old believers but even those that are new

You see sometimes things get so dark

And the consequence of our sin has left its mark

Even then our heavenly Father remains with us

So just turn around return to Him and don't fuss

Friends and love ones may run away

But we can be confident, the Holy Spirit is here to stay

What God says He means my child

Do not let Satan cause you to live in pride

When you feel like you can't make it no more

Don't rely on your feelings, close that door

Your will is stronger than your feelings you know

So, look at it in God's way and your attitude will show

That you understand the verse in Romans 8 when God said

'All things will work for your good' Believe that instead

Listen as I advise you to learn Psalm 121

That is a great psalm to meditate on

Reminding you to look up to The Lord for help always

He controls everything till the end of days

He doesn't sleep, his phone is never dead

He is in fact waiting for your call instead

He will preserve you from all evil

Your sleep will be sweet not harassed by the devil

Let me remind you about what He says about you and me

We are seated in heavenly places, now through eternity

We are more than conquerors so we must trust

If God be for us, who can be against us?

He has given us everything we need for godliness and life

And will always cause us to triumph in Jesus Christ

If you keep chewing on that verse you will never feel low

In fact, in your speech, attitude and thoughts you will glow

Greater is He that is in you than He that is in the world

The bible says to believers both young and old

I can do all things through Christ who strengthens me

He gave it all up without our having to pay a fee

Without a doubt if you take this advice

You'll find yourself drawing nearer and nearer to Jesus Christ

THE OMNIPOTENT GOD, SEEN IN THE STORM

Have you ever heard the thunder roll after the lightning flash?

Our Great God Jehovah is responsible for that celestial crash

Is there anything He cannot do?

For you and you and you and you?

The meteorologist can only follow the storm

And report as the weather changes on and on

They cannot stop a hurricane in its pathway

But only inform us as it moves day by day

That should cause all the world to see

The Omnipotence of God of heaven and agree

That He is able to do the impossible for you and I

Whatever is your problem don't despair and cry

When the seas are raging

And large raindrops are falling

When the sky becomes pitch black

And men run for cover before the attack

Know that God is not unaware

For He can stop it with one word, no need to fear

This piece was written especially for you

Who are going through a storm and don't know what to do

Call on the God Who walks in the storm

Be sure as you believe He will perform

That which you have called on Him for

Just look closely for that open door

That He will surely create for you

He is always present and well able to see us through

THE AWESOME GOD WE SERVE

Who is this God that you serve?

Is He the One Who spoke and things came into being

Creating the moon, stars and everything seen and unseen?

Is He the One Whose handiwork we see in the sun and moon

Who is coming back for us very soon?

Is He the God of Abraham, Isaac, Jacob, David and Moses

The Merciful, Gracious, Omnipotent, and Faithful One of all ages?

Is He the One Who caused food to fall from the sky

And sent His only Son to die for you and I?

Is He the One Who opened the Red Sea

And brought His people over to victory?

Is He the One Who cannot tell a lie

His Word has been proven true, on it we can rely

If He is the same one you serve today

Then always look the part in everything you do or say

Don't let the enemy back you in a corner in this Year

Believe everything that God said, you hear?

Keep your hope high in God my brethren in Christ

Hope gives you room to fall and get up, Isn't that nice?

God has given us so much to work with

And many have problems believing it

He's given us everything we need for life and godliness

It is His gift to us; we must take it and use it

There are so many things given that we have to put on

Including the armour to fight the devil to scorn

God gave it to you; you have to put it on, yes!

That is how you'll get the victory in every test

Know that you are definitely an over-comer

Protected by angels, called of God and more than a conqueror

God always cause us to triumph in Christ Jesus

That is why we are all still in the race, so don't make a fuss

No weapon that is formed against us would prosper, know that

But Satan and his imps will continue to launch their attack

If these demons stay faithful and consistent on their job, why can't we?

When attacked, use the Word of God and Jesus' name and make them flee

Our faith is what will overcome the world

Faith is believing God, relying and adhering to Him, will make us bold

We are so blessed to have Jesus Himself interceding for us

Singing, praising, dancing and rejoicing in Him is a must

The joy of the Lord is your strength, keep that in mind

Through the days keep your joy and your strength all the time

Sometimes you may cry, that all a part of the race

Bottom line, make sure you see Jesus' face

And hear Him say "well done my child

No more crying, now wipe your eye dry"

So, when you are tempted to be depressed

Count your blessing and you'll pass the test

You might be surprised at what the Lord has done for you

And how many people will willingly exchange places with you too

Let us all seek to pass every test in and shine

And use the talents God gave us to encourage others all the time

Doing everything without murmuring, grumbling, complaining or fault-finding

Just seek to please God by obeying Him in everything

Take this free advice and things will be fine

When the drum rolls and Jesus shows up, you will not be left behind.

PRAISES TO THE MOST HIGH GOD

Sing praises to the Most High God

All you people who call Him lord

For He spoke and things came into existence

He commanded and they stood firm without resistance

He sees the hearts of all people on the earth

Every one of us whom He made from dirt

He upsets the plans of peoples and nations

But His plans stand firm forever in every generation

Let us never be ungrateful to our God

But continually praise Him in one accord

Sing praises to the Most High God

He showed His love for us by giving us Jesus our lord

What more do we want Him to do?

Since His love remains intact for me and you

He left us His word so we will know how to live

Our love and obedience to Him we should give

Yet some people take His blessings and grace

With no regard for what He requires us to face

We cannot fail; of this we can be sure

His Holy Spirit is given to us to close sins' door

Sing praises to the Most High God, I implore

Jesus is seated at His right hand for sure

Praying for us as we live this life on earth

It is something for which we should take note

When we come together in His holy name

Lift your hearts and hands, it is not in vain

For He sees our hearts we cannot fool him

Let us be grateful for His forgiveness of our sins

Forget the person standing next to you

In fact, encourage them to know Him too

He requires us to praise Him, are you aware of that?

It is in His word many times that is a fact

Many people praise everything else they love

Except the Almighty God Who is from above

Manufactures praise their products all the time

Fans praise their sporting heroes every time they shine

One cannot stay still when they hear a skilful musician play

So why is there a problem in praising God every day?

Let us praise God who gives us the air we breathe

Don't let the rocks take your place, fill that need

I SEE GOD IN A PLANE RIDE

I see God plainly in a plane ride

As the plane go high, high up in the sky

Oh, the wisdom God has given to man

To use the aerodynamics of birds to get the plane off the land!

It is amazing to watch this iron object fly

Pulling its wheels up, my oh my

The birds carry up their legs too

As they spread their wings to let the wind through

I see God plainly in a plane ride

As I l look through the window in the sky

Everything on earth diminishes as the plane shoots up like a rocket

No wonder Isaiah says 'God sees the nations as a drop in a bucket'

One comes to terms with the insignificance of man

For men beat their chest when they have money and land

I see God clearly in a plane ride

With the vast expanse of sea and sky

As the plane rise above the clouds

God is really magnificent and amazing no doubt

His grandeur and excellence are seen

Clearly in creation, it is no dream

God is awesome people hear me

Don't play with sin do like Joseph and flee

The next time you or one you know rides in a plane

Meditate on the Omnipotence of God again and again

HAPPINESSS! WHERE IS IT FOUND?

Do you really want to be happy as ever?

Find you own happiness in yourself through God's power

Quit depending on someone else to make you happy, yes

Keep your eyes on Jesus, trust in God, and be at rest

No human being on earth can create that for you

Be complete in yourself through God, that is true

Why allow what someone else does to destroy your life?

And cut you up spiritually as if with a knife

Why permit the actions of another to rub you of peace and joy?

Jesus died to give that to you not any man, woman, girl or boy

Look at life right in the eye and say

I'll not allow anyone to drag me down from today

I'll discover my own source of happiness of course

No more leaning on someone, Jesus is my boss

Meaning and purpose to life comes from Him

Not an ordinary human like myself liable to sin

Know that your needs are spiritual, not physical

Once our basic needs food shelter and clothes are met

Our greatest need is spiritual until death

Ask the rich man who seem to have it all

And is usually the one who takes the hardest fall

As he reaches the top of his game

And finds no satisfaction with riches and fame

Scores of movie stars we admire

Have the money and fame many desire

Yet many are on drugs and others commit suicide

Those are lessons we can glean from and not die

Paul said God shall supply all my needs

According to His riches in Christ Jesus, so take heed

Not your husband, wife, pastor or best friend

Will be able to give you happiness to the end

Eventually you must get rid of every crutch

And learn to call on no one but Jesus

Of course, get counselling from those mentioned above

But in the final analysis listen to me my love

They would only help, if they make you do it on your own

Take your need to the Lord, He will help you not leave you alone

IF GOD DID IT BEFORE, HE CAN DO IT AGAIN

Why fret believers? Why worry my friend?

If God did it before He will do it again

So now you are sick and lying in bed

Don't let the enemy put lies in your head

You have testimonies of what God did before

And if you want others, I can give you some more

Did He not heal you before this time?

When people come to visit you, strike up a lime

About the faithfulness and power of God today

To heal the sick, even raise the dead if intensely you pray

Why fret believers? Why worry my friend?

If God did it before He will do I again

So now you're broke, or your money runs low

Don't let you mind be fixed on things here below

Continue to tithe and give generously my friend

Believers are aware of how that sacrifice will end

With God pouring out from the windows of heaven above

Don't fret and worry, He will come through for you love

He is able more than able to accomplish what concerns you today

He took money from a fish mouth, that's all I have to say

Why fret believers? Why worry my friend?

If He did it before He will do it again

So, your children or spouse not behaving as they should

Giving you unending heartache as an enemy would

Would worrying and quarrelling fix that sister and brother?

Keep your mind and heart on God's word is better

It will save you from getting sick or having a nervous breakdown

So, wipe your tears, see your BIG God and remove that frown

He is competent reliable and faithful all the time

Rejoice evermore, pray without ceasing and His joy you will find

FAITH IN GOD

Faith is being sure of the things we hope for

Knowing that something is real even if you don't see an open door

This poem would look at men and women of faith

Who can inspire us, and of whom we can relate?

A pillar of faith was Noah a great man

He built a large boat with his own hands

Simply because God told him to

He did not need any other reason like me and you

Abraham, the father of us all

Was a great man of faith, he obeyed God's call

He had no idea where he was going

But that did not deter him he went without hesitating

For he believed God when a promise is mentioned

It did not matter how impossible the situation

Though he was very old he expected a child

Because God's Word is never denied

Moses' parents hid him for three months by faith

Such a beautiful child, no one should hate

They were not afraid to disobey the king's orders

And his mother got to look after him, for God grant her favour

Moses refused to be called the son of Pharoah's daughter

Choosing to suffer with God's people thereafter

Rather than enjoying sin for a short time on stage

He left Egypt not being afraid of the king's rage

There were many more who died in faith

Time will not permit me to relate

But the list of them makes me conscious of

The mercy and forgiveness of the Great One above

David, Samson and the prostitute Rahab too

Joseph and Isaac are the names of a few

Believers, please take God at His Word

Faith is the belief that our prayers are heard

Do something that demonstrates faith too

For faith without works is dead, it's the bible's point of view

Be Challenged

GOD IS NOT MOCKED!

It started way back in the Garden of Eden

With Adam and Eve, the only two people then

The woman was deceived and the man was not grieved

So, God made them leave

The whole creation was cursed and bound

The woman, man, serpent and ground

The serpent was cursed with a crush for his head

The woman, child bearing pain will make she see red

The man had to work for his daily bread

Or he and his family sure starve till they dead

But God remained as Lord, as Judge and as King

For He is Almighty and reigns sovereign

Then came the era with Noah and his boys

Noah tried to warn the people but they mocked him with noise

They were eating, drinking and making merry

When God poured down water in great fury

They rushed, run, fall to the ground

They attacked the door with so great a pound

But too late, too late was the cry for them

God in His righteous judgment washed them away to the
end

For God is not mocked my friend

The cry against Sodom and Gomorrah was great

Homosexuals running rampant through the gate

Our great God looked down from on high

And was so grieved, He sentenced them all to die

In His mercy he saved Lot and those belonging to him

For it is God's nature to help the faithful in suffering

Our great God rained down burning sulphur

Every man woman and child burned to a cinder

God is not mocked he is the great I AM

He is fire, sulphur, water but also a lamb

Now we are in the 21st century time

Jesus paid the price we didn't put a dime

The cost was His life on Calvary's cross

So that men will be saved and none will be lost

But what some people try to do instead is mock God

But He will treat them dread, dread, dread

They lying, cheating, and hating and unforgiving

But only watching fornication and murder as sin

With God it ain't have none of that

Big sin and small sin, all in the same hat

Let us be careful to do His perfect will

In sincerity, honesty and love everyone still

Our Great God is still watching be sure

When He is finished with mockers, there won't be a cure

ARE YOU WALKING IN DARKNESS?

God is Light, in Him there is no darkness at all

If we say we have fellowship with Him and walk in darkness

We lie and do not the truth, and are in danger of a great fall

Whoever says he is in the light and hates his Christian brother

Is in darkness even right now

Repent, repent you are in danger of hell fire

The darkness some people walk in is unbelievable

It has blinded them and sin seems innocent and enjoyable

Take this quick bible check with me

And decide if you are on the road to see the Jesus of Galilee

All that is in the world is the lust of the flesh

That is the craving for sensual gratification at best

The works of the flesh are very clear

Galatians 5:19 spells it out for us, so hear

They include sexual immorality and impurity

Like Joseph this temptation should make us flee

Why are you continually having sex and you're not married?

And fooling yourself thinking you don't need to take heed.

But you are walking in darkness, beware!

Let the truth of God's word shine through and change your ways, you hear?

Lasciviousness and debauchery are two big words saints

Simply meaning indecency, absence of restraint

You do what you want, when and how you want it too

That is part of our sinful nature, it is nothing new

Witch craft, which is also sorcery and idolatry

Are also part of the darkness, hear my plea

The obeah house is no place for you to go

And then come to church and put on a show

God is not mocked, time to wise up now

If you don't know, the pastor or other believers will show you how

If you are a hater, causing enmity and division

You are walking in darkness and false religion

Jesus commands us to walk in unity and love each other

Not gossip, backbite, evil talking, strife and slander

Jealousy, anger, envy, fits of rage

Will always put you on centre stage

For people to speak evil of all believers in God

Imagine you behaving so and calling Jesus Lord

It is amazing how Trinbagonians' carnival mentality

Has crept into the church, you'll all agree

The works of the flesh that causes walking in darkness

Drunkenness, revelling and carousing is on the list

The latter means lively or noisy drinking party my dear

Where participants drink alcohol heavily with no care

 The word of God does not condemn having a drink

As so many Christian people will have us think

But the warning is that wine is a mocker and strong drink
is raging

And whoever is deceived by it is not wise, no joking

This should make us stop and check ourselves and
choose

Singing praises and being filled with the Spirit and not
booze

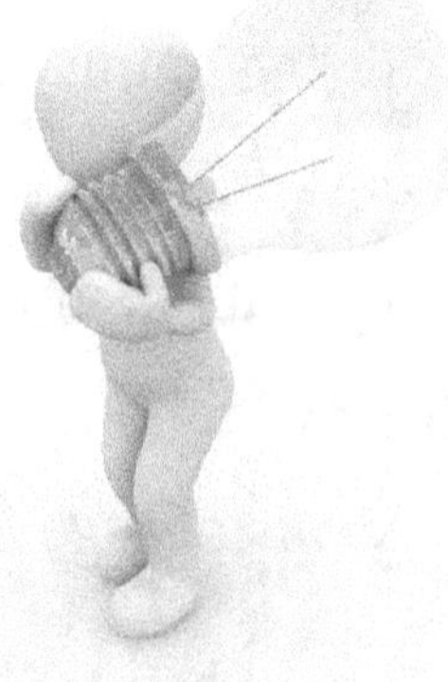

WHEN YOU FEEL LIKE GIVING UP

Problems, problems, problems everywhere, everyday

Positive thinking alone doesn't make them go away

When a wife shed tears watching her marriage break up

And she stands by powerless to make it stop

Remember not all marriages are helped through prayers or good intentions

Ask the many divorcees or those experiencing separation

It takes two to make a marriage work

And a partner could resist the Holy Ghost's conviction, no joke

Many have had thought giving up at times, I'm sure

But why do feel this way? What is the cure?

What to do when temptation rolls over like a flood?

Do I give up? Quit? Never! I lean on God

There is great comfort in two things I learnt

The first is God really loves me; I'm never on my own

Not a sparrow falls to the ground without the Father knowing

Matthew 10: 29 is where you see those words glowing

God did not give up on King David when he fell

His involvement with Bathsheba, the story we know well

Second, know the Lord never gives up on any of us

So, we should never quit, staying focus is a must

Even if you feel wounded, hurting, lonely and lost

Your faith in God is what pleases Him most

Don't let Satan turn your blessings into a curse

Revelation reminds us to put God first

Accept the love of God and keep your faith strong

Know that believers are praying for you all along

DON'T PLAY WITH SIN!

Be alert and watchful, don't play with sin

Keep your spirit clean within

Set your mind on things above Paul says

To live a true Christian life all your days

Sin will cause you to miss God's best

And not live pure, holy lives above the rest

Sin will paralyse some and others may die

When we listen to Satan and obey His lies

Don't settle for being a mediocre Christian

Let's be excellent, just as our saviour commands

Even at times when we may fail

God's love grace and mercy is to our avail

Dust your feet, get up, continue to fight!

With every battle in the Holy Spirit with all your might

What is the state of your mind my friend?

What you think about will be your end

As a man thinketh in his heart so is he

Think as God instructs us and like Him we'll all be

Satan is a liar and will try to blind your mind

With problems you face and trouble on every hand

Cast down every imagination and every high thought

That exalts itself above what God says, bring that
thought to nought

Lying, gossiping, and backbiting are not the only sins

With ugly thoughts and impure motives, you'll never win

So, I plead with you with all my heart

Hold on to Jesus as you did from the start

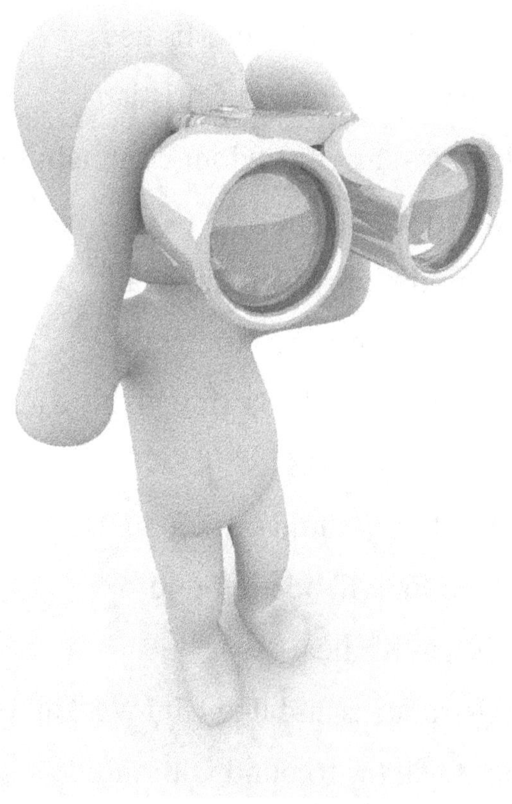

YOUR FAITH WILL BE TESTED

God has given to every man the measure of faith

The just shall live by faith to enter heaven's gate

For without faith, it's impossible to please God

But He is a rewarder of them who seek Him as lord

Do you know in the Old Testament the word faith occurs only twice?

And never once the name Jesus Christ?

Old Testament faith was never mere assent to doctrine

But utter confidence in the faithfulness of God and not kin

I want to warn you that your faith will be tested for sure

Just as Abraham's Noah's and Joseph's and Job's did

The genuineness of your faith which is more precious than gold

Will be tested and purified by fire so we are told

Bringing praise, glory and honour to our God in heaven

It's recorded in first Peter chapter one verse seven

The proving of your faith brings out steadfastness and patience

So that you will be not lacking having much resistance

To Satan, the devil the enemy of our souls

The bible tells us brothers and sisters that we should be bold

So, prepare yourself my brothers and sisters all your days

Difficult situations are sometime used to learn God's ways

Let me encourage you to stand fast in trials now

Our faith will overcome the world that's how

God always cause us to triumph in Christ Jesus

We are more than conquerors through Him that loved us

Greater is He that is in us than He that is in the world

That's a main truth in scripture we need to behold

He who has begun a good work in us will complete it against that day

The same Spirit that raised Jesus from the dead indwells us the Word say

I hope these few reminders will stay with you

And cause you to have victory in all that you do.

ENDURING TO THE END

Hebrews 12 encourages us to run the race with grace

Not giving up until we see Jesus' face to face

The Christian race is not a jog you know

But one that is demanding and taxing high and low

Sometimes it can be a distressing race

And the enemy taunts you in your face

It will take immense effort to finish strong

If you take your eyes of Jesus, you will not last long

There are many who started the race and turn back

And now stands watching at the side of the track

There was a time when they kept the pace

And depended solely on the Lord's grace

But weariness stepped in and they had enough

Never thinking the race will be so tough

They had a bout of sickness or got distracted by the world

And allowed Satan to squeeze them into his mould

They retired before their time you know

Their best work was their first work to show

Many have been discouraged by fellow runners too

Their hearts are not in the race anymore, believers take
a cue

They attend church service and give of their funds

They sing in the choirs, dance and speak in tongues

But when they leave church, they put on a different face

No one will believe they were in the Christian race

That is where we who are still running in lane

Should try to help them not to sin again

Jesus' strongest step was His last step, so know that

Even though the devil launched his lethal attack

He obeyed God to the point of death

Looking beyond His immediate pain, His face set

Knowing His sacrifice will bring life to others

We are the beneficiary of His agony brothers

So, when going through your difficult time

Be obedient to God, let your light shine

See how others can benefit from your battle

Looking beyond your pain to someone else's gain

REMINDERS TO YOUNG MEN

God calls young men because they are strong

Therefore, live righteously and never be wrong

I know God's Word must come to pass

But I don't expect men of God to be in the class

Of being lovers of themselves, covetous or without
natural affection

But loving God giving Him His just, due attention

Let's examine the life of young men in God's word

Then talk to other young men, let your voice be heard

David the young shepherd boy, the son of Jesse

Is good example for us all to see

Looking faithfully after His father's sheep

He had a rod and staff in hand they did not bleat

He killed a lion and a bear with his hands

He knew in those fights God was in command

David believed in God with all His heart

And he was able to quench the enemy's fiery darts

He slew Goliath the giant we all know

With a sling and a stone, not a gun, or bow and arrow

Whatever is in your hands Father could use

If you will consistently obey and not refuse

David said to the giant, "I come in the name of the Lord"

The opportunity is there for you to stand tall in God

Joseph was a young man I truly admire

His testing was as hot as fire

Young men try to put yourself in his place

People who are supposed to love you can betray you in your face

You end up in a place you did not cater for

But your love for God kept your heart pure

So instead of plotting revenge when you come through

You thank Almighty God for being there for you

You recognize the enemy meant to do you harm

And used those closest to you to work his charm

You see everything Joseph dreamt came through

I wonder what the prophets have spoken about you?

Guard that word, God will surely bring it to pass

Just keep your mind and heart fixed on Him down to the last

Bloom where you are planted and, in that place

Don't dread the trials and inconvenience you face

See them instead as springboard for promotion

Character developers that purify your thoughts and actions

God can and will change your circumstances so don't fuss

But first He's going to use tests to change all of us

Young men, don't give up, but go through

God is standing in your corner, He loves you

BEWARE OF THE FALSE DOCTRINES

The bible warns to be aware of false doctrines today

This is something believers must take seriously I say

If it were possible even the very elect will be deceived

But with the Holy Spirit inside that cannot be achieved

This poem will just address one such doctrine

About believers not having to ask God forgiveness for sin

It is said that Jesus paid for our sins once and for all

So, we don't need to repent again if we fall

They say we are under grace not law

And that is true, we need not go through that door

Grace allows us to go boldly before God's throne

Not just to obtain mercy and get help alone

But they forget 'without holiness no man shall see God'

That is something that cannot be ignored

In the book of Romans, we Gentiles are addressed

Being warned not to put God to the test

Because if He cut off His chosen people for disobedience

What make us think He will do any different?

The Israelites were put away because of unbelief

Sadly, not believing what God says is on the increase

Read the whole account in Roman eleven from verse seventeen

And tell me if this doctrine isn't the most ridiculous ever seen

We are also being told to ignore the Our Father prayer

That Jesus gave to us His followers so dear

Because it says " forgive us our trespasses..."

And we are already forgiven when we were saved

They forget in the letters to the seven churches in revelation

Believers were told to repent, let me have your attention

The over comers were also given special awards

As Jesus listed the works that were not in accord

With what He expects of believers who accepted Him

Beware believers repent and don't let your light grow dim

Do like David and ask God to search your heart

Get your sins washed away as you did from the start

This poem is written just for you to be like the Bereans

And cross check everything you hear today friends

RAHAB

God is marvellous, amazing and can make anyone new

Ask Rahab, her story is recorded in the bible just for you

What about her, what is her history? one may inquire

To tell you about her is my greatest desire

A woman of questionable character, a prostitute

She harboured enemies of the then authorities to boot

And when questioned she gave a bold face lie

What is she doing in God's holy word? one may cry

Don't be too quick to judge her I say

Hear the end of her story and be amazed today

This woman of whom one might have been ashamed

To be connected to their family and spoil its good name

But check the information you're receiving in Joshua chapter two

See how God can change anyone who connects with Him for true

Matthew chapter one verse five and six reveals some important facts

She was King David's great, great grandmother, take that!

This notorious woman's story does not end here

She was in the lineage of our Saviour Jesus, get it clear

So, it is important that you don't judge people at all

You may be standing or sitting next to a modern-day apostle Paul

If you think this poem is ending here you are wrong

This woman story could make other women very strong

Sister Rehab's name is mentioned in Hebrews 11:31 pray tell

As a woman of faith who was saved when the walls of Jericho fell

Joshua chapter 6 verse 7 records that information, go check it out

It can result in your life being enhanced or completely changed no doubt

And in James chapter 2 verse 25 her works are recorded too

Her works of rescue were given as evidence of her righteous faith do

Go around to the various churches and ask questions and you will find

God turned many into beacon of righteousness so now, you stand in line

YOU CAN SURVIVE!

Some folks have heard negatives all their lives
Their minds are filled, they only live to survive
From the vicious attacks from people in their sphere
Even those they love and hold in their heart so dear
When one is attacked from their loved ones at home
The stinging words that pierce their hearts alone
Can destroy their self-esteem sometimes forever
Let's be careful of what we say sister and brother
If you are one who feels left behind
This poem is to encourage you, you can shine
Potential does not have an expiry date
Pick yourself up and start it is never too late

When important people in your live discard you
Sad to say including some teachers too
When they say you are dunce and can't learn
Don't believe it! Kick it out of your zone
You are much more than any label can define
In fact, God created you with gifts to shine
It is a tragedy some people never discover their gifts

The way the education system is designed perpetrates this

For though the way people are wired to learn is not fixed

You have to sit behind a desk from kindergarten to form six

Those that get out and learn a trade before adulthood

Are among the few who make it while many others should

Let me share with you what science now says

This is the latest information given by Dr leaf today

Neurologically, you are not wired for someone else's gift

But the education system in T and T is yet to understand this

So many people are becoming certified paying minimal fees

With degrees from bachelors and Masters to PHDs

But not functioning effectively in the workplace

I think that I have a very good case

Sitting for years behind a school desk is partly responsible for this

Students from the early stages should have a diagnosis

highlighting efficient and effective methods for individuals to progress

And not just to pass a pen and pencil test

Students must not be promoted if they can't read

That is basic skill every citizen need

So let me get right back on track

This poem was not written for that

But continue to tell you what science now say

And assist you to get up and try again today

You are not your scores, don't ever believe that

That is a recent proven scientific fact

Each person can do something no one else can

Many progressive people started late became successful too man

Eisenstein was diagnosed with a learning disability that set

And there were many others you have not heard about yet

But he beat the odds when he understood all too well

We were all wired differently but can succeed and others tell

He found the key and opened the door that tried to box him in

Listen people get up again, try once more singing a song

That shows those that dismiss you as a failure that they were wrong

Acknowledgement

I wish to thank God for bestowing me with the gift of writing simple poetry and monologues to promote His Kingdom.

I wish to thank my husband, Michael, for his love, patience, unstinting support and listening ear. I love you.

I wish to thank my pastor, Apostle Irvine Celestine, pastor of HELPS and Deliverance Int'l Ministries in Point Fortin, who was the final voice to propel me into writing and publishing this book of poems.

Finally, I wish to thank my family, friends and all my brothers & sisters in Christ who encouraged me to write time and time again.